VIETNAM
OUR WORLD IN COLOUR

VIETNAM
OUR WORLD IN COLOUR

Photography by Sarah Lock
Text by Stephen Bull

The Guidebook Company Limited

Copyright © 1993, 1991 The Guidebook Company Limited, Hong Kong

Reprinted 1993

All rights reserved, no part of this publication may be reproduced or transmitted in any form or by any means, electronic or mechanical, including photocopy, recording or any information storage and retrieval system, without permission from the publisher.

Photography by Sarah Lock
Text by Stephen Bull
Edited by Nick Wallwork
Series Editor: Caroline Robertson
Designed by Patrick Ma

Printed in China

ISBN 962-217-120-6

INTRODUCTION

VIETNAM forms an elongated 'S' shape which has often been compared to the ubiquitous bamboo pole carried on a woman's shoulders as she goes to market, creaking under the weight of the produce balanced on either end. The pole represents the narrow central strip which joins north and south, and the two weights represent the rice fields—on one end, the Red River Delta (Bac Bo) and on the other, the Mekong Delta (Nam Bo).

For it is on these two vast alluvial plains that the majority of Vietnam's food is grown and where the majority of its 70 million people live. Most of the remainder live along the country's 2,900 kilometre (1,800 mile) coastline, so along with rice, fishing is very important in terms of both labour and diet. Three-quarters of the country is thinly populated jungle and highland.

As anyone who has driven the length of the country will testify, most roads run from north to south and rivers from east to west, so it is a case of many rivers to cross—sometimes on rickety bridges which have been patched up since the war, but more often on an array of primitive but ingenious ferry boats.

With the capital Hanoi and major city Ho Chi Minh City (formerly Saigon) 1,600 km (1,000 miles) apart—three days by train—it is not uncommon to meet southerners with no experience or conception of life in the north and vice versa. Not surprisingly, this has made the post–1975 task of reunification all the more difficult.

But if Vietnam's shape is inexpedient, its overall geographical location most certainly is not. Wedged between Southeast Asia and the Far East, the Vietnamese find themselves in the midst of the planet's most dynamic economic region. For political reasons, the country continues to be bypassed where wealth-creating regional trade is concerned, but this surely cannot last for long. The Vietnamese are intelligent, skilful, resourceful and hardworking by nature. It may now be the fourth poorest country in the world, but it lacks many of the fundamental problems confronting, say, a landlocked and arid African country. The future, it seems, can only be brighter. One certainly hopes so, for if ever there were a victim of twentieth-century world history then Vietnam—through no particular fault of its own—would surely be it.

Recent changes suggest this beautiful and deeply fascinating country is all set to become a major tourist destination. But as it is only just emerging from a long period of war and isolation, the immediate future is unlikely to produce an easy-going, laid-back tourist paradise like Thailand. Vietnam is more for those who like their travel to be challenging and are prepared to put up with moments of discomfort and bureaucratic confusion in return for a rewarding, other-world experience. Its inclusion among 'holidays for thinking people' adverts may continue for some time.

Neither is Vietnam really the place for those who like exploring ancient ruins, temples and pagodas, for it has a secular Confucian past and cannot compete with Burma and Thailand when it comes to magnificent Buddhist architecture. Moreover, and with few exceptions, what might have been visited—for example the Citadel at Hue—was either badly damaged or destroyed during the war.

Enter the concept of war tourism and the possibility of visiting another type of ruins. The world is still fascinated by this small country which did a David and Goliath act on the greatest military power ever known. Subsequent films about the war may only have been told from an American perspective, but they have succeeded in maintaining interest. The authorities are not unaware of this, and military miracles such as Dien Bien Phu, the Cu Chi tunnels and the Ho Chi Minh trail are being developed for the purpose of tourism. In any case, the personal anecdotes are there for all to hear, and the burnt-out tanks, damaged environment and profusion of cemeteries remain for all to see.

(Top)
Patriotic poster celebrating the 100th anniversary of Zthe birth of Ho Chi Minh.
(Above)
Fishing boats at Nha Trang.

It is a reflection of foreign involvement in Vietnam—and of the history of tribal conquest in the region—that it is sometimes difficult to talk clearly in terms of a Vietnamese culture. All previous occupants have left their mark, but none more so than the Chinese. For over ten centuries their attacks from the north had to be beaten off, the most recent skirmish being the 1979 border war. The social and cultural residue of this long and vexed relationship is omnipresent, so much so that in some ways, Vietnamese culture is indistinguishable from that of its powerful neighbour.

Confucianism as a conservative system of government came from China to Vietnam very early on. It involved the dynastic rule of an absolute monarch (the 'Son of Heaven'), via the institution of the mandarinate, over a network of largely autocratic and self-governing villages.

Despite recent contact with Western ways, Confucianism as a religion and way of life is still very much in evidence today. The practice of ancestor worship and notions of filial piety and duty to the family co-exist with responsibilities to the party. Fatalism and stoicism continue to be marked characteristics of the Vietnamese people—the philosophy of withdrawal and endurance of hardship are a sign of those who believe that the future is determined according to the mandate of Heaven and not the individual resolution of contradictions.

Which is not to say that the Vietnamese are incapable of acting for change, for like the Chinese, they are fascinated by fate and fortune (i.e. geomancy, spiritual consultation, fortune telling, Taoist sorcery, astrology and even gambling) and though they are inclined to bend with the wind, they can act with extraordinary determination if they sense that destiny is on their side.

The Vietnamese language has borrowed thousands of words from the Chinese and until this century the Chinese script was used extensively in academia, and a scholar would be brought up on the Confucian classics. At the same time though, there has been a rich vein of national consciousness running throughout Vietnam's history which has given rise to an enduring and often bitter rivalry. From the Trung sisters onward, the definition of a Vietnamese hero was one who had fought off the Chinese. A street map of any town or city will reveal some of the names—Ly Thuong Kiet, Tran Hung Dao, Nguyen Hue, Le Loi and many more.

If the concept of Indochina has any meaning at all, then ethnically speaking, it could be said that Vietnam represents the 'China', and Cambodia and Laos the 'Indo'. For the Vietnamese share with the Chinese a similar diet and a fair complexion, whilst the Lao and Khmers bear a closer physical resemblance to Indians and a Theravada Buddhist tradition which places them alongside the Thais and Burmese. That the three countries became a confederation last century was of French making, rather than a reflection of shared characteristics.

French forces first landed at Danang in 1858, and control over the three regions of Tonkin (north), Annam (centre) and Cochin China (south) was compelled in 1883, but in fact, French missionaries and traders had entered the country as early as the seventeenth-century. Indeed it was a French cleric, the Bishop of Adran, who helped Gia Long to crush the Tay Son rebellion and establish the Nguyen dynasty in 1802. The French brought many desirable things to Vietnam, although few would regard their *Mission Civilatrice* as wholly positive and their presence struck deeply at the roots of Vietnamese civilization, resulting in a profound shift in the social fabric.

'Moral' society was replaced by 'productive' society and the need for surplus and profit. This created a merchant class, and once–cultured mandarins turned into the corrupt government officials that were to plague the country for many years to come. Together they brought the pressures of the outside world cruelly into hitherto isolated and autonomous villages, whose respected notables (whether elected or not) alienated themselves from their people by becoming the agents of the merchants, government officials and the newly–defined national economic needs.

It was a French missionary, Alexandre de Rhodes, who transcribed the alphabet from Chinese ideographs into Roman letters. This may have been an assault on local culture, but it made Vietnam more able to integrate with the outside world. More significant than this perhaps, was the introduction of a French education system, which created a class of people who were Western in outlook.

Today, most reminders of the French presence are of the charming variety. For example, the names of some imports have crept into the Vietnamese language, such as *ga* (railway station), *pho mat* (cheese) and *oto* (car).

Generally, the French legacies are dwindling rapidly, and that applies to those few people who can still speak French, as well as to the fleets of the Renault *Saviem* buses which still ply some of the rural routes. Then there are the yellow villas in tree-lined boulevards, often with green shutters leading out onto balconies with pots of brightly coloured flowers. The paint may be faded and peeling, but the origins are obvious.

The Cathedral of Notre Dame in Saigon is red brick, not Gothic, but unmistakably European and among the most important places of worship serving Vietnam's estimated six million Catholics. Next door, the post office is a majestic colonial structure; inside, a portrait of Ho Chi Minh looks whimsically down on the noisy proceedings.

French cuisine has also left its mark—from espresso coffee to pâté to crispy baguettes. Even Maxim's restaurant is still there in Saigon, where excellent value dishes are served by highly trained waiters in waistcoats and bow-ties. The atmosphere, enhanced by a string quartet, is from another age.

After Dien Bien Phu, the Americans began to arrive in ever increasing numbers, culminating with the landing of combat troops at Danang in 1965. Needless to say, evidence of their presence is confined almost entirely to the south. The differences which still exist between the north and south are epitomized by male headgear. Northern men wear the austere and very sober pith helmet, their more freewheeling southern counterparts, the American baseball cap, often sporting an advert for some obscure mid-Western garage or burger bar.

The Americans came with their democratic ideals, dollars, bombs and ill-conceived ideas such as the attempt to relocate thousands of villagers away from their sacred land (regardless of the fact they were severing ancestral ties) and then wondered why they were unpopular. Their sense of mission created a logic which could destroy towns like Can Tho in order to 'save' them. As Graham Greene said of one CIA operative, 'I never knew a man who had better motives for all the trouble he caused.'

The Vietnamese are making good use of the baseball caps and many other leftovers. A burnt–out tank near Dong Ha makes an ideal playground for the local children, whilst a lot of other useless military hardware is being sold off as scrap metal to Japan. A typical roadside bicycle repair man keeps his tools in an upturned GI helmet, and the 'American Market' in Ho Chi Minh City is still selling off new and used US military paraphernalia.

Southern Vietnam is like a museum of 1960s expressions and Vietnamese-English phrase books can still be found, though phrases like 'Don't Shoot!' and 'You wanna have fun soldier?' no longer come in very handy. It is as though time froze in 1973—most GI bars are long gone, but there is still one in Saigon which has black and white prints of Hendrix, Joplin and Morrison staring down at the clientele.

Until recently the saddest reminders of the American presence were the hordes of outcast Amerasian children roaming the streets. A huge and lucrative service industry

(Top) *'Floating restaurant' selling meals to houseboats in the Mekong Delta.*
(Above) *Old Chinese–style junks fishing on an estuary of the Red River.*

(Top)
A White Thai minority girl from a mountain village close to Dien Bien Phu.
(Centre)
Poultry seller in Cholon, the Chinatown of Ho Chi Minh City.
(Above)
The traditional straw hat provides excellent protection from the sun.

grew up around the US camps and the kids were a testament to the oldest service industry of them all. With the passage of the Amerasian Homecoming Act in 1987, the US assumed responsibility for them and almost all have now been resettled.

In a country which suffered so enormously at the hands of Western military might, it is quite extraordinary to see posters of macho idols like Rambo selling quite openly on the streets, and not easy to reconcile the ambivalence between a people who are proud of their Viet Cong war heroes, but who also maintain a scarcely concealed admiration for America and the whole GI culture.

Vietnam's most recent foreign visitation was an altogether more low-key affair. Apart from the occasional official passing in a black Volga, there was not much visually to suggest that Vietnam had become the Eastern bloc's foothold in Southeast Asia, since technicians and advisers were asked to keep a low profile.

Of course, the Soviets never invaded Vietnam, but it would be wrong to say that they and their European Marxist philosophy have not exerted a great influence on the country. Of the two Western systems used during the period of partition, it is perhaps communism that has fitted in more easily with Confucian orthodoxy. Neither Confucianism nor Marxism promote an entrepreneurial class and both reject the notion of individualism. For the mandarin, read the party bureaucrat; for the self-governing village, read the cooperative; and for fate and the mandate of Heaven read the historical process and dialectical materialism.

The Soviets contributed significantly to the post-war renovation of Vietnam's industry and agriculture, but also exported their own crippling style of management and inefficiency. Likewise, the bureaucracy and security apparatus are run on Soviet lines. Those who visited the Soviet Union would recognize immediately the languid, at times downright perverse official procedures. Perhaps unfairly though, the Soviets acquired the tag 'Americans without dollars'.

In spite of foreign penetration, Vietnam has succeeded in maintaining a strong sense of nationhood and absorbed elements of foreign civilizations without losing its own identity. Indeed, prior to the Chinese annexation in 111BC, the Vietnamese had an original civilization of their own—a kingdom centred around the Red River basin and known as Au Lac. The Viet as a tribe are of uncertain ethnic origin, but are probably a mixture of Central Asian and Indonesian stock.

With Chinese domination cast aside in AD939, there followed centuries of almost uninterrupted independence. The longest lasting dynasties were the Ly (AD1009-1225), Tran (AD1225-1400), Le (AD1427-1789) and Nguyen (AD1802-1945), although after 1883 the Emperors were under the control of the French.

During the Middle Ages, the Viet moved slowly southward from their northern homeland, eclipsing the kingdom of Champa and giving rise to Vietnam as we know it today. The Champa civilization dated back to AD200 and finally fell to Le Thanh Ton in AD1471. The Cham, of Malay–Polynesian origin, were pushed back from central Vietnam right down to the Mekong Delta. There are still traces of Cham civilization today; ruins can be visited and some aspects of Cham culture (e.g. its theatre, music and art) can be detected in Vietnamese culture. A tiny minority of Cham still live in the south, but most ended up in Cambodia, where they were almost completely wiped out by the murderous Khmer Rouge during the late 1970s.

In addition to Chinese and Khmer minorities, Vietnam has around sixty hill tribes who live in the highlands bordering Laos and China. Almost all are animists and are of either Malay-Polynesian or Mon-Khmer stock. Some have always lived in these areas, others retreated there during the southward push of the Viet. They suffered terribly during the Indochina wars, and many were forced to leave the land of their ancestors. Numbering less than one million people, the hill tribes live on the margins of Vietnam society. The main tribes in the south are the Rhade, Jarai, Sedang and Bahnar; and in the north, the Thai, Muong and Meo.

Apart from these animist peoples, some Vietnamese are atheists and some Catholics, but the overwhelming majority would call themselves Buddhists. Over the centuries though, the Confucian royal court never promoted Buddhism (but they certainly did not outlaw it either) with the result that for many, it became fused with Taoism and Confucianism into a vague code of ethics and a philosophy of life rather than a practised religion.

But there is one religious sect in southern Vietnam which is totally unique. Begun in 1929, Cao Daism sums up the varied religious influences on Vietnam into a fascinating body of spiritual beliefs which comprise elements of Buddhism, Taoism, Confucianism and Christianity. The sect was well known during the 1950s because it ran a private army and worshipped the spirits of European heroes like Victor Hugo, Joan of Arc and William Shakespeare, receiving messages from them during seances.

Interestingly, the Cao Daist hierarchy is modelled on Catholic lines, with bishops and priests. Their headquarters, or Holy Sea, is a large estate near the town of Tay Ninh centred around a bizarre looking Cathedral which Norman Lewis referred to as, 'A fantasy from the brain of Disney'.

The spirit of Cao Dai is represented by the 'Universal Eye' which is painted above the entrance to all Cao Dai churches; it first revealed itself as the 'Universal God of Mankind' during a seance. Its followers have claimed that this is the religion to unite all religions but insofar as Cao Daism is also a social and political phenomenon, it can be seen as a typically Vietnamese quest for harmony, an attempt to reconcile the conflicting forces that were tearing society apart in the French period. Even today, the sect is thought to have around two million adherents.

Of the three major cities in Vietnam, Ho Chi Minh City is the economic powerhouse, a city which lives by its wits and fascinated a generation of Frenchmen and Americans. Hue was the capital of Vietnam under the Nguyens and the Annamite capital under the French. Lying on the banks of the beautiful Perfume River, its Citadel, containing the Forbidden Purple City was almost totally destroyed by a fire in 1947 and by fighting in 1968. The royal tombs on the edge of the city are well worth a visit.

Then there is Hanoi, the ancient capital which has risen again and is the resting place of Ho Chi Minh, the father of modern Vietnam. The city exudes a dreamy austerity and stoicism, where misery and the urgent task of day-to-day survival seem to co-exist with an unhurried contentedness and frugality. Images of Hanoi which spring to mind are of a man sitting on the front step of his rundown house, teaching his son how to play classical guitar, and of a young couple on a park bench in the gathering dusk making the act of holding hands seem as profound as it possibly could be.

Sadness permeates most aspects of life in Vietnam—it can be seen on the faces of the people (mingling in with the smiles) and heard in their poems and popular songs. For the Vietnamese, poetry is the most noble form of expression. Along with proverbs and legends, poems have been handed down over the centuries and nearly everybody knows a few lines from the best known of all, Nguyen Du's *Kim Van Kieu*. This is an epic of 3,254 verses which at once praises and questions the notion of filial piety. Above all it is a sad and romantic story of unfulfilled love. The following story, *The Beautiful Angler*, by Nguyen Hoai Duc says a lot about the sentimental and the romantic ideals of the Vietnamese.

(Top)
A cyclo driver looking for a passenger in Hanoi.
(Centre)
A view over Ho Chi Minh City of the Continental Hotel and Cathedral.
(Above)
Taxi drivers in Dalat.

(Top) *Water buffalo are used throughout Vietnam for ploughing and other tasks.* (Above) *Pumpkins on sale in a market in the Mekong Delta.*

Her hair, escaping from the jade comb, floated in the wind. She had finished her sowing and spinning and, wandering off towards the river she came and leaned upon a stone wall. Her heart freed from the cares of the house, she amused herself by fishing. Drawn by the divine perfume which enveloped her, a myriad of butterflies came to alight on her rod, weighing it down until it almost touched the water. Frightened by her miraculous beauty, the fish disappeared to the bottom of the stream, leaving the bait to drift away. It was only for her pleasure that she fished. She took no heed of her lack of success. And when she drew in her line an automatic sadness seemed to spread across the waves.

Vietnam is well acquainted with the pain of love, and not just of the romantic kind, for love of country runs very deep. The post-war dream—or even assumption—that the heroism and genius of the war effort would be reproduced in peacetime happiness and prosperity remains a dream, tragically unfulfilled. The tendency to grin and bear it is strong though, in fact it is a question of honour. Also high on the list of virtues in Vietnam are politeness and modesty to the point of shyness. A pleasant lie is often preferred to a harsh truth. Boasting and loss of temper are not approved of, subtlety and self-control most certainly are. But these are the poor attempts of a Westerner to make sense of what he has experienced.

It was once said, that, 'Culturally, Vietnam is quite beyond the normal range of occidental comprehension,' and implied that Vietnam and China are the most Asiatic of Asian countries. Judging by the vexed attempts of the French and Americans to come to terms with what they were trying to do there, this is borne out by the facts. Vietnam has a mystique which rarely fails to baffle and intrigue. A classic example of the mixed reactions it can provoke was illustrated when President Kennedy dispatched two senators to Vietnam to assess progress on the rural pacification policy. On returning, one report suggested that things were going very well and that the South Vietnamese government and the Americans were very popular. The other said that the scheme was doomed to fail and that they were roundly hated. A puzzled Kennedy called the two men into his office, asking 'Were you two gentlemen in the same country?!'

> Vietnam today is still a very poor country; its plight has not been helped by the withdrawal of Russian and East European aid. But its future is more hopeful than it was. The Communist party is tentatively releasing its control over the economy. The effects of this move are, as in China, most obvious in the south. Ho Chi Minh City is bustling with entrepreneurial activity; stalls and shops are spilling over the pavements, whilst Asian businessmen are crowding the bars and restaurants. Furthermore, with the relaxing of entry requirements, more and more tourists are experiencing this beautiful, sad, otherworldly country. And with them come tourist dollars. Ordinary Vietnamese see the greatest obstacle to development as being America's Trading with the Enemy Act which still, over 15 years after the war, imposes a trade and aid embargo on the country. The feeling now is that America will soon relent. The signs are that another of Asia's little dragons is about to find its feet.

Villages are a hive of activity during harvest time. Threshing machines such as the ones pictured are rare, and tractors are even rarer, so the traditional, labour-intensive methods are still very much in evidence. Food production has nearly doubled in the ten years since the government began experimenting with private enterprise by allowing farmers to lease plots of land for limited periods. After meeting their quota, farmers are allowed to sell their surplus on the open market.

(Above)
The fields in the valleys in the mountainous region of Son La Province are a glorious patchwork of gold and green.
(Right) *Traditionally the women of the village carry out the back-breaking tasks in the endless cycle of planting and harvesting the rice.*

Anti-clockwise from opposite page
A young girl takes vegetables to market. Using the traditional sling-and-bucket system, mother and daughter (opposite top) *scoop water from the channel to irrigate the paddy fields.* (Above and top right) *An alternative method, using cycle-powered water wheels placed over the channel, is employed for the same purpose.* (Centre right) *A young woman tends to her spring onions—often mixed with garlic and spices, they are used as a garnish in* pho, *the rice–noodle soup which features strongly in the diet.*

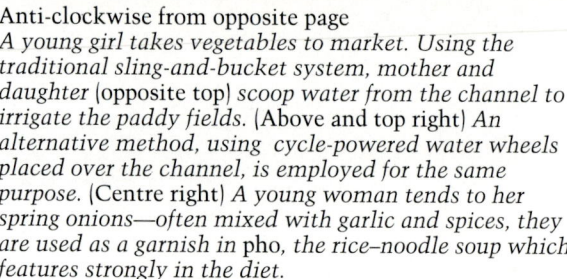

Vung Tau is an important seaside and fishing town, and being only 128 km (79 miles) east of Ho Chi Minh City, is a popular destination for Vietnamese tourists. Known as Cap St Jacques by the French who built seaside villas as weekend retreats, its golden beaches rimmed by coconut palms made it a popular R & R resort for American GIs during the war.

Early in the morning the women meet the fishing fleet on return from a long night's fishing to help unload the catch and then take it to market. (Above) Minor repairs and repainting are carried out during the day's low tide. As the tide comes in, passage to and from the fishing boats is made in circular, woven boats.

Vung Tau. The fishermen's morning is spent unloading their catch, haggling over the selling price, and sorting their nets in preparation for another night's work.

The Westerners may have left, but their mark remains indelibly stamped on Ho Chi Minh City, formerly Saigon, the South Vietnamese capital. The French legacy is most apparent in the elegant architecture found throughout the city.

(Above) *Ho Chi Minh City People's Committee, the seat of the city government, formerly the Hotel de Ville. The interior of the Central Post Office (right), designed in 1896 by the French architect Villedieu, is dominated by a huge portrait of Ho Chi Minh. Reflecting the country's present political stance, overseas letters are separated into those going to socialist and non-socialist countries. (Below) The imposing red-brick St Maria Catholic Cathedral, commonly known as the Notre Dame Cathedral.*

(Left)
Rush-hour traffic on Le Loi, one of the main streets in Ho Chi Minh City. There are few private cars in the city, but an increasing number of mopeds are appearing on the streets.

(Below) *Sunset over the Saigon River from the roof of the Cuu Long Hotel, formerly The Majestic. The new Floating Hotel on the left is a sign of Vietnam's increasing popularity both as a tourist and as a business destination.* (Right) *Reunification Hall, formerly known as the Presidential Palace, was the headquarters of the South Vietnamese Government. It is recognisable from the famous film footage showing an NLF tank crashing through its iron gates, effectively marking the end of the war.*

(Above Left) *Saigon Opera House.* (Above right) *View from the roof garden of the Rex Hotel, a popular haunt of journalists during the war.* (Top) *Ben Thanh, or Central Market, where a curious variety of luxury items from abroad, including Russian caviar, German beer, 'Levi' jeans and Japanese stereos are on sale.*

(Above right) *Amerasian children with their mothers. The US has offered to take all who wish to leave, and few now remain.* (Bottom right) *'Luxury' food items from abroad can be bought in the streets near the port, obtained on the black market, from sailors.* (Bottom left) *The French have left, but the baguettes and pâté have remained.* (Top left) *Street vendors appear early each morning to sell breakfast to people on their way to work.*

(Top) *A cyclo driver helps an old lady arriving for the Sunday morning service at the Notre Dame Cathedral, presided over by the Bishop of Saigon. The present Bishop (above) is the first Vietnamese to hold the title, his predecessors having been French.* (Right) *Many people exercise in the early morning, before the heat of the day.*

Funeral wreaths and footwear illustrate the traditional Vietnamese flair for colour and beauty. Red is considered an auspicious colour and is used lavishly throughout Vietnam, being both the colour of the communist party and the colour for prosperity and wealth.

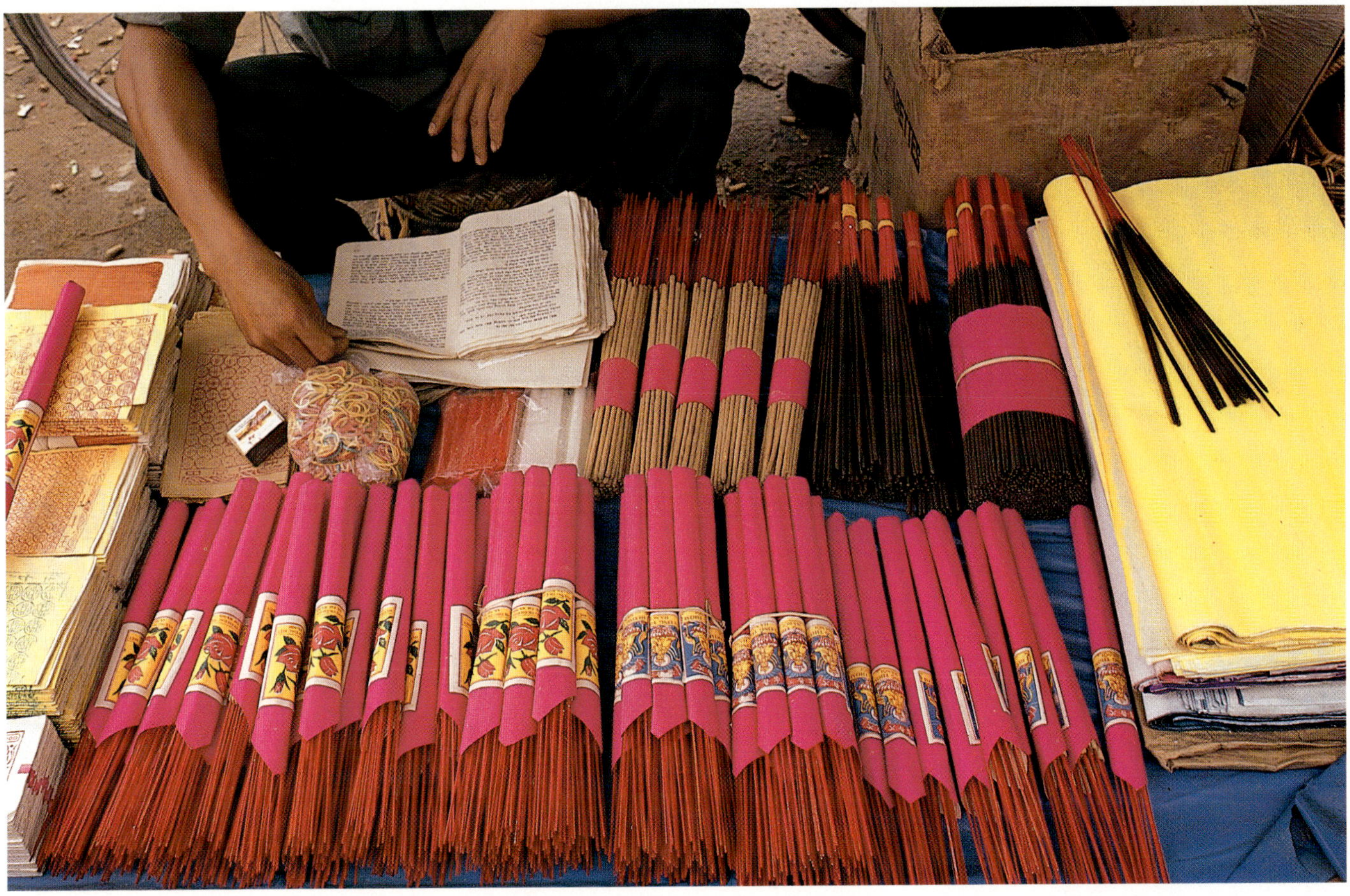

60
ĐI LÊN CHỦ NGHĨA XÃ HỘI
LÀ CON ĐƯỜNG TẤT YẾU CỦA NƯỚC TA

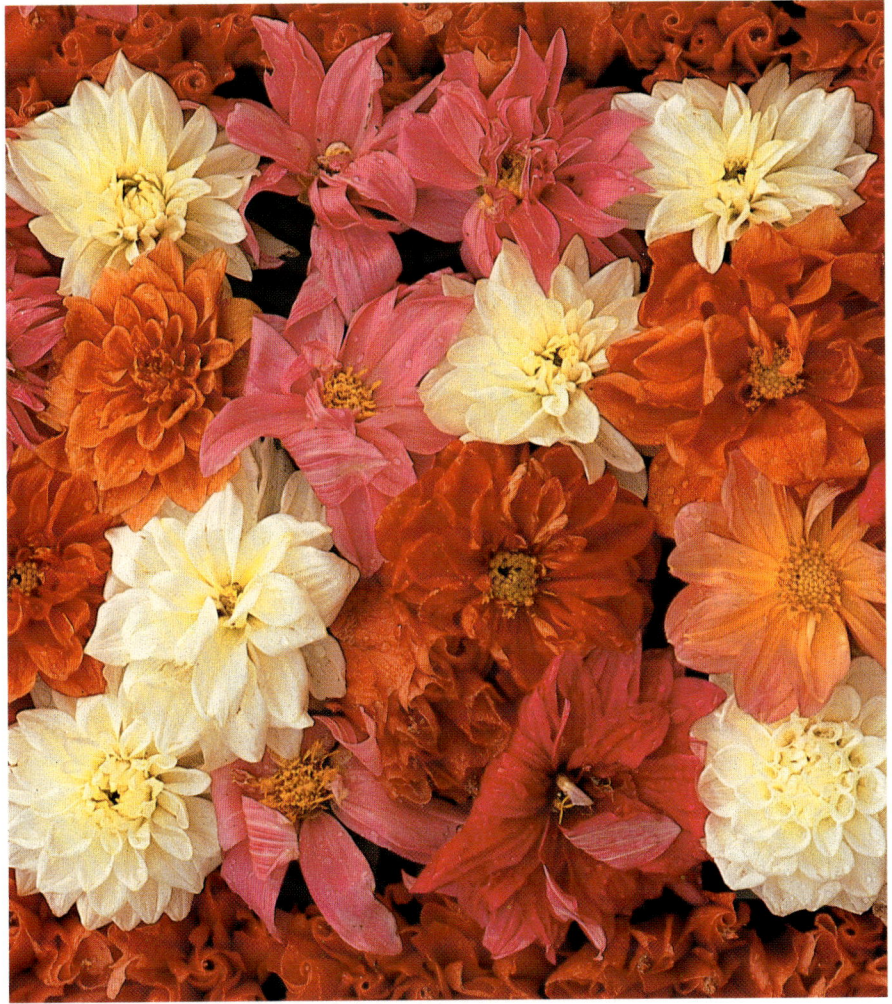

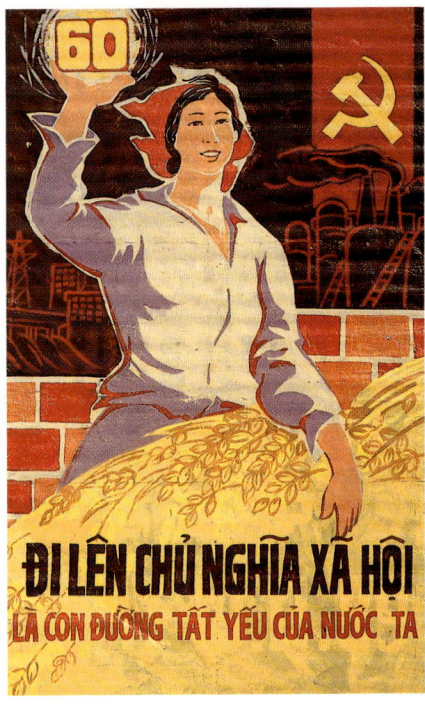

(Above) *View from Highway One north of Nha Trang, in central Vietnam.* (Top right) *Defoliants, such as Agent Orange, dropped by the Americans in the war resulted in devastation of large areas. The climate in the mountainous regions of Vietnam provides conditions suitable for the production of tea* (right) *and coffee.*

(Left) *The mineral rich soils near Dien Bien Phu are washed into the surrounding rivers during the monsoon season, turning the waters a startling shade of pink. The monsoon season lasts from May to October when an average of 300–400mm of rain falls each month making access to villages like the one below almost impossible.*

Nha Trang, with its beautiful beaches and picturesque setting, was a popular R & R centre for Australian and US troops. Under the shade of the palm trees, people sit at the small cafés and sip iced coffee (Opposite page).

(Above) Farmers from plantations upriver travel along meandering tributaries to sell their produce at the marketplace in Nha Trang. (Right) In the shelter of the harbour, fishermen spend hours checking their nets in preparation for a night's fishing.

Following pages
The Old Quarter of Hanoi, Dong Kinh Nghia Thuc, named after a great revolutionary cultural movement, is a labyrinth of tiny streets selling everything from traditional herbal medicines to the ubiquitous pith helmet.

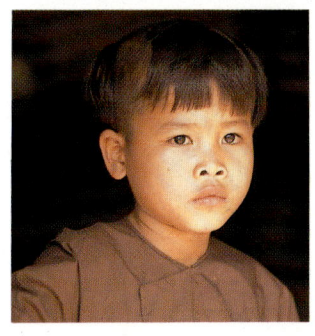

Buddhism is the religion of the majority of Vietnamese, into which concepts from Taoism and Confucianism have been incorporated.

(Left) *A Buddhist ceremony at the Vinh Nghiem Pagoda, built in 1964, the largest and most modern in Ho Chi Minh City.* (Top) *A Buddhist service for college students, dressed in their white uniform of* ao dai, *and school children at a small temple in Dong Ha.*
(Above left) *Buddhist nuns studying religious texts at a pagoda in Ho Chi Minh City.*
(Above right) *A young monk at the Thien Mu Pagoda in Hue.*

(Left) *Beautifully embroidered silk banners hang in the dark halls of the Thien Mu Pagoda on the banks of the Perfume River.* (Above) *The Chinese pagoda of Fuc Kien in Hoi An is testimony to the long association of China with Vietnam. The town was established as a base for Chinese traders in the fifteenth-century.*

(Above) *Brightly coloured billboards reflect the political atmosphere.*
(Left) *Political dogma and religious reverence are combined in a temple poster incorporating Ho Chi Minh.*

Dalat was established as a hill station by the French to escape the heat of Ho Chi Minh City for the cool mountain air. Once called La Petite Paris, *its romantic ambience attracts young lovers and honeymoon couples.*

(**Above**) *The climate in Dalat is conducive to the production of a wide variety of vegetables and fruits which are sold in the market. Some, such as strawberries, were introduced by the French and are used in the production of wine and strawberry jam.*

(Above) *Amid the pine forest of Dalat, a typical French–style weekend chalet.*

Opposite page
River life outside Danang.

(Left and below) *Wrapped for protection against the harsh effects of wind, salt and sun, women labour in the salt fields along the coast close to Nha Trang.*

The faces of Vietnam.

The pattern of colour constantly changes throughout the cycle of planting and harvesting.

(Above left) Children are given the task of minding the buffaloes while they graze. (Left) Minority women wade through a swollen river on their way to market.

Hue, the ancient capital of Vietnam, is a city of pagodas, temples and royal tombs. Established six hundred years ago on the banks of the Perfume River, many of its ancient relics are still in excellent condition despite saturation bombing by the Americans during the war.

(Above left) *The East Gate of the Imperial City, which was composed of the Royal Citadel* (below left), *the Imperial Enclosure, and the Forbidden Purple City, the former residence of the royal family.*

(Above and below right) *Gateways leading to the tomb of Minh Mang, emperor from 1820 to 1840. A much respected leader for his emphasis on Confucian traditions and his encouragement of new agricultural techniques.*

Civil and military mandarins, elephants and horses guard the tomb of Emperor Khai Dinh who ruled from 1916 to 1925, during the French colonial period. The bizarre architecture reflects elements of both cultures.

Opposite page
Market scene at Can Tho in the Mekong Delta. The variety of produce in the markets of the Mekong Delta reflects the fertility of the area which produces more than enough rice to feed the south and central parts of the country. Markets are the life-centre of every town and village.

The town of My Tho in the Mekong Delta suffered badly during the war. The US Airforce dropped thousands of gallons of defoliants in the area. It is once again a busy river thoroughfare with individual family boats on the outskirts giving way to the ferry and commercial traffic in the centre of town.

Duck farmer tends to his flock.

63

On 8 March 1965, 3,500 US marines landed on China Beach, Danang, marking the United States' active entry into the war. (Below) *View of Danang from the Hai Van Pass.* (Left) *'Mother of the Hero', a statue made from melted-down American shellcases.* (Centre left) *A patriotic billboard.* (Bottom left) *Japanese pagoda built on the bridge in Hoi An in the seventeenth-century, to appease a large water monster that created havoc in the area.*

The Kingdom of the Chams arose in the late second century AD. The death of the last Cham king, Po Phan Pi, in the late eighteenth century triggered an exodus of Cham descendants to Cambodia. However, many still live in the provinces of Nghia Binh, Phu Khanh and Thuan Hai.

(Top)
Cham Tower, close to Quy Nhon in Nghia Binh province. The museum in Danang houses Cham sandstone sculptures from the fourth to fourteenth centuries.

(Below) *Vendors work on the ferries that ply the Mekong supplying newspapers and local snacks.* (Bottom) *Left by the Americans, battered old Dodges and Cadillacs still lumber around the streets of the south. They are used as taxis accommodating families of up to fifteen.*

On 11 June 1963, Thich Quang Duc, a 73-year-old monk from Hue, burned himself to death in protest against government persecution of Buddhists. At his home pagoda of Thien Mu, the car that carried him to Saigon is preserved, inside of which is a copy of the famous photograph of the act which shocked the outside world.

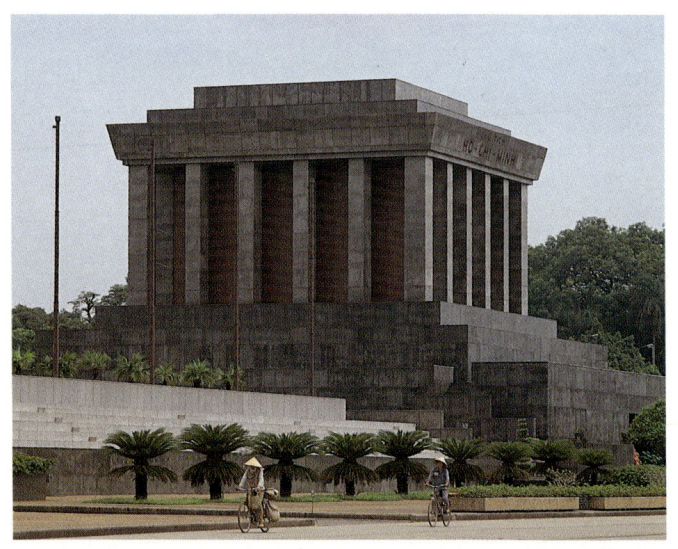

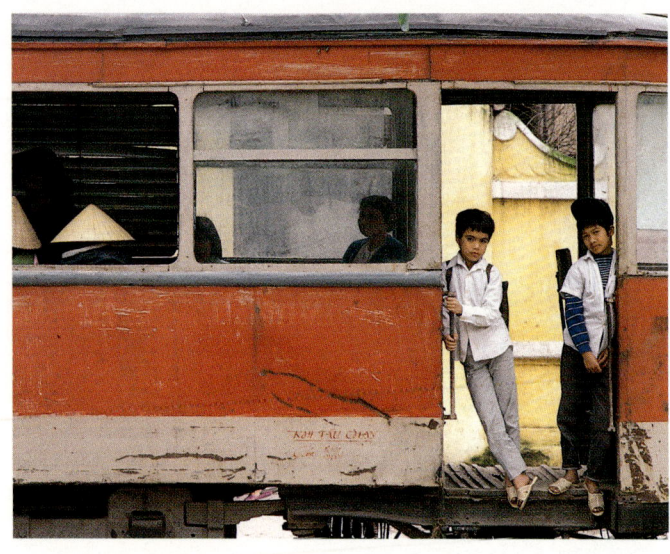

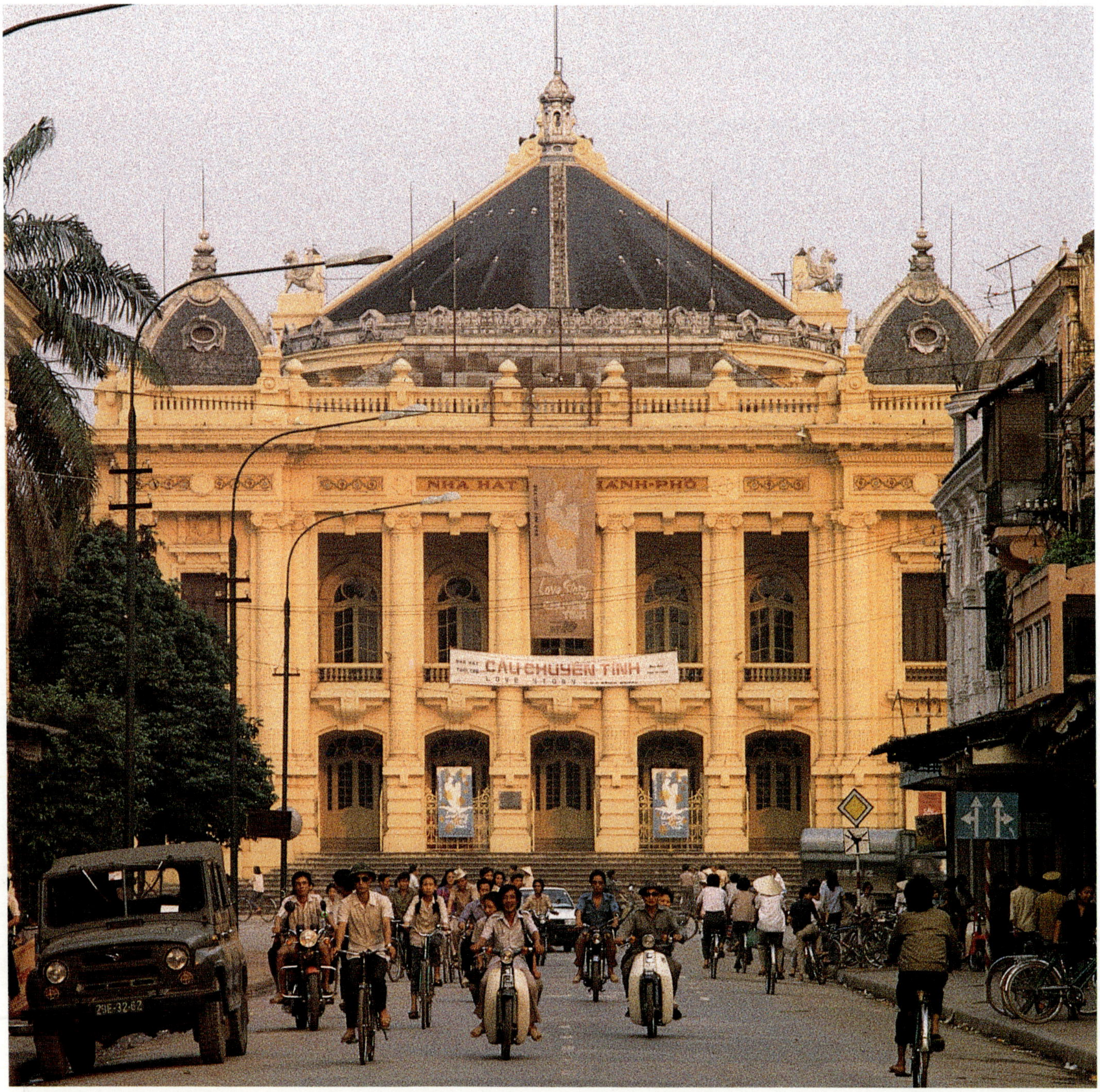
NHA HAT
ANH-PHO
CAU CHUYEN TINH
LOVE STORY
29E-32-62

Hanoi, the capital city of the Socialist Republic of Vietnam, has retained much of its old-world charm. The city was a seat of the colonial government of French Indochina from 1887 to 1957 and many fine buildings from this period still survive. (Opposite below) The Opera House in Hanoi displays all the elegance of French colonial architecture. (Opposite, top) Ho Chi Minh lives embalmed in his mausoleum, a site of pilgrimage for Vietnamese people. Dilapidated old trams still trundle through the streets of Hanoi. (Below) Wartime relics such as helicopters, planes and rockets are now used by children in an amusement park. (Below right) Outside Hanoi railway station, cyclo drivers wait for passengers.

A variety of scenes of Vietnamese life, in the labyrinth of the Old Quarter of Hanoi.
(Above) An ear masseuse who, with his array of equipment, produces different sensations.
(Centre left) Tailors of made-to-measure imitation Levi's. This whole street in Hanoi makes copies from a few old pairs salvaged from departing American GIs.
(Bottom left) Eating pho in a local restaurant—a popular soup with rice, noodles and shredded meat seasoned with lemon and chilli.
(Left) Typical French shuttered doorway.
(Right) A portrait artist working in his roadside studio.

(Above) *Sandals made from recycled tyres as worn by Ho Chi Minh, even when meeting foreign dignitaries, to show his solidarity with the Vietnamese people.* (Anti-clockwise from far left) *Army surplus in Hanoi. A Buddhist shrine at a temple in Hoa Lu, the capital of Vietnam AD968-1010. Fresh fish for sale at a roadside market. 'Dragon in the Clouds' mural on the ceiling of the Tomb of Khai Dinh in Hue.*

(Left) *Detail from a temple carving in Hoa Lu.* (Below) *Posters express the genuine reverence and affection felt by the Vietnamese for Ho Chi Minh.*

Many Vietnamese converted to Catholicism during French rule. The Catholic church is incongruously the dominant feature of many small villages. (Opposite page far left) *Grain drying outside a Catholic church near Nha Trang.* (Below left) *Tombs in the Buddhist cemetery in Dalat incorporate the swastika and miniature portraits of the deceased.* (Top left) *The Cao Dai sect incorporates beliefs from Confucianism, Catholicism, Taoism and Buddhism, which are represented in the painting at the entrance of every church.*

(Below) *The spectacular setting of this Catholic church north of Hanoi enhances its simple splendour.*

Of the 54 ethnic groups in Vietnam, the minority races constitute 7 million people or ten percent of the population. Residing mainly in the Central Highlands and the mountainous regions of the north, they were referred to as montagnards by the French.

(Opposite page below left) Traditional houses of the White Thai minority are raised on stilts to protect them from flooding. Their wealthy status, derived from the gold they pan in the surrounding areas, is reflected in their beautiful costumes (opposite page above right, right and below right).

Close to the Laos border on the Ho Chi Minh trail live the Bru Van Kieu minority (opposite page left and bottom right).

Many of the minorities are related to those in Thailand, Burma, Laos and China, such as the Meo (above) and Muong (below).

An A To Z of Facts and Figures

A

Ao Dai A beautiful and ever-so-slightly tantalizing traditional female costume now worn mainly by hotel receptionists, bank clerks and the like. A close-fitting, brightly-coloured silk top with a revealing slit on either side of the midriff, worn over long silk pants.

Annam Referring to the central region of Vietnam, and including the imperial capital of Hue, Annam was ruled by the French as a protectorate.

Au Lac The name of northern Vietnam under the rule of the Hung Kings. In 2BC Au Lac was conquered by the Han Chinese and ruled for 10 centuries after which the country became known as Dai Viet.

Adran Bishop of Adran, otherwise known as Pierre Pigneau de Behaine. An eighteenth-century Catholic missionary and explorer who was responsible for arousing French interest in Vietnam and who helped Nguyen Anh (later Emperor Gia Long) to put down the Tay Son rebellion and establish the Nguyen dynasty.

Amerasians Those born of Vietnamese mothers and American fathers during the war. As far as Vietnam is concerned, an increasingly rare breed, since most have now left for the United States.

Agent Orange A defoliant used by the US military during the war to expose the enemy. Around 50 million litres were sprayed in all, containing 170kl of dioxin. The effects on human health and the environment were devastating.

B

Binh Xuyen An armed gang run by the notorious Bay Vien, which came to prominence after the Second World War. They ran protection rackets, opium dens, casinos and brothels and contributed to Saigon's sordid image. Eventually they were seen off by President Diem.

Bao Dai The last in line of the Nguyen emperors, he abdicated after the Second World War. A weak leader and renowned playboy.

Buon Me Thuot This town in the southern Central Highlands is the capital of Dac Lac province and has a very well attended Catholic church. The province produces the best coffee in Vietnam and is well known for its elephant races and parades. The town is also a basecamp for visiting villagers of the area's 31 different ethnic minorities —in particular the Rhade and Muong tribes.

Bargaining Much appreciated and delighted in by traders, unless you take it too far. Remember Vietnam is a very poor country.

Bo Doi A Vietnamese soldier. Until recently, the country had the fourth largest army in the world.

Black Lady Mountain Near Tay Ninh. A mysterious and impressive looking hill (mountain-like because it stands out in an otherwise flat landscape) with a network of caves which once housed the Cao Dai arsenal. Run by left-behind Kuomintang soldiers, the caves were later used as a hideout by a Cao Dai breakaway group under General Te.

C

Coastline Plenty of it. Over 2,900 kilometres (1,800 miles) stretching from the hills of Quang Ninh province bordering China's Buanxi province to the Ca Mau peninsula west of the Mekong Delta, where the town of Ha Tien borders with Cambodia's Kampot province.

Currency The *dong*, roughly 10,000 to the US dollar (mid-1992). Traveller's cheques are convertible in Vietnam, but credit cards hardly so at all. To exchange or send money go to the Bank of Foreign Trade in Hanoi or Saigon. Money transfers may take up to a month and can only be cashed in *dong*.

Cyclo A three–wheeled pedicab. Cheap and enjoyable way to get around towns.

Cholon Originally a neighbour of Saigon, this is Chinatown and now lies within districts 5 and 10 of Ho Chi Minh City. One time hub of southern commercial activity—and a den of iniquity—it was subdued by the revolution but is now showing signs of a return to life.

Cao Dai A syncretic religious sect based near the town of Tay Ninh. Its beliefs represent a strange mixture of Buddhism, Taoism, Confucianism and Christianity. Followers worship Cao Dai, a spirit thought to be the 'Universal God of Mankind', and Victor Hugo and Joan of Arc are included among the sect's minor saints. The Cao Dai, who used to be a political and military force during the 1940s and 50s are still very much in evidence today.

Cochin China A name originally given by the Portuguese (as distinct from Cochin India) which the French later used to describe the southern third of the country which they ruled as a colony from Saigon.

Cu Chi 30 miles north-west of Ho Chi Minh City. An extraordinary network of tunnels used by the Vietcong during the war as a hideout and secret village. The scene of some dramatic battles with a crack US squad known as the Tunnel Rats.

Cheap Charlie Old wartime expression and what southerners are likely to call you if you bargain too hard—or can't afford what they expect you to afford!

Cham A Muslim and one time Hindu tribe from the south whose Kingdom of Champa was obliterated by southward Vietnamese expansion. There are Cham remains to be found in the Nha Trang/Danang area, as well as some Cham people. In Cambodia, the Cham were almost completely wiped out by the murderous Pol Pot regime.

Chay Vong Vong A bizarre Sunday night ritual in downtown Ho Cho Minh City. Thousands of motorbikes and bicycles drive round and round in a never–ending flow, which can make crossing the road dangerous if not impossible.

Conical Hat Traditional but still very much used peasant hat which reflects the sun and shades the face.

D

Doi Moi The Vietnamese equivalent of *perestroika*, it literally means 'renovation'. The policy was introduced during the sixth Party Congress in 1986.

Dien Bien Phu A highland village in the north-west near the Lao border, and scene of France's last stand in 1954. The French were encircled and eventually routed by the Viet Minh under the brilliant leadership of General Vo Nguyen Giap.

Dalat A French hillstation discovered around 1893 by Dr Yersin. The area has clean, cool air, numerous waterfalls and lakes and inspiring scenery. Dalat, which is a favoured destination for lovestruck young couples, poets and dreamers, was largely spared during the Vietnam War. Tea and mulberry as well as fruits and vegetables grow well here. Many ethnic minorities live in the hills of Lam Dong province, particularly the Ma and the K'hor.

Danang (formerly Tourane) Immortalized as the point where American combat troops first landed in March 1965. Less well known is that in 1858, this was also where French forces began their campaign. Nearby My Son was the holy city of Champa, and there is an interesting Cham museum in Danang. The city is overlooked by the Marble Mountains, which have a Buddhist monastery and caves that were used by the Vietcong as a hideout. Danang was an important airbase during the war and of course there was the notorious R & R hangout at China Beach.

E

Ethnic Minorities Around 12 percent of the population. Principally ethnic Chinese and Khmer, Vietnam also has around 60 hilltribes, many of whom were plains dwellers until forced into the hills by the Viet and Cham expansion. Under the French, the hilltribes were know collectively as *Montagnards*. They have struggled under successive regimes to maintain a separate identity.

F

Fan Si Pan Vietnam's highest mountain, 3,143m (9,580ft) high. It is situated near Sa Pa in the northern province of Hoang Lien Son.

Festivals Tet or Lunar New Year is at the end of January or the beginning of February. Firecrackers, unicorn dances, family gatherings, gift exchanging etc. (The celebrations in 1968 were overshadowed by the Tet offensive, a massive Vietcong attack on southern strongholds). The Children's Festival in mid-autumn includes lantern parades. Many villages still have a peace ritual, invoking the local guardian spirit. Also, festivals connected with the arrival of Spring, the spirit of rice and the harvest. The anniversary of victory at Dien Bien Phu is 7 May; 28 July is Invalid and Martyrs' Day; and 30 April commemorates the liberation of Saigon in 1975.

Flag The national flag is a red rectangle with a five pointed gold star in the middle.

Food Vietnamese food is similar to Chinese but usually more spicy. Seafood abounds of course. Try in particular, *cha ca* (fish fried in cumin and served with vermicelli), *ghai gio* (Vietnamese spring rolls) and *nuoc nam* (fish sauce). French food has also left its mark.

Flights Vietnam Airlines, with its fleet of ageing Tupoles and Illyushins is known as Hang Khong (rudely referred to by some as Hang On Airlines), and serves all major cities. Apart from connections to Eastern Europe, there are, at the moment flights to Bangkok (on Thai Airlines and Air France), Paris (Air France), Manila (Philippine Airlines), Jakarta (Garuda), Singapore (Lufthansa and Garuda), Kuala Lumpur (Malaysian Airlines) and Hong Kong (Cathay Pacific).

G

Gia Long The royal name of Nguyen Anh, who was crowned as Emperor of a united Vietnam at Hue in 1802. This was the beginning of the Nguyen dynasty which lasted (but nominally under the French) until the abdication of Bao Dai.

H

Hoi An Just south of Danang, this small town used to be called Faifo, the point where European settlers first landed in Vietnam. The Portuguese established a trading post here in 1535.

Handicrafts Vietnam's best known product is lacquerware—mother-of-pearl designs laid into lacquered wood (usually ebony). Also, embroidery, bambooware, reed baskets, pottery and woodwork.

Hanoi Formerly Thanh Long, it first became a capital as far back as the eleventh century. Located in the heart of the Red River basin, it has beautiful parks, lakes and tree–lined boulevards. Hanoi has a very austere, not to say rundown atmosphere. See in particular: the Ho Chi Minh Mausoleum, the History and Revolution Museums, the Two Sisters and One Pillar Pagodas, the Temple of Literature, the Hoan Kiem (Restored Sword) Lake, the Hanoi Hilton (prison which housed American POWs) and last but not least, the old town consisting of thirty–six lanes, most of which are named after particular trades.

Hoa Binh South-west of Hanoi in Ha Son Binh province. A stopping–off point for visitors to Dien Bien Phu and hilltribes such as the Muong, Thai and Meo.

Hue One time imperial capital which holds a special place in the hearts of all Vietnamese and is still known for its poetry, scholarship, and apparently beautiful girls. Lying on the banks of the Perfume River (*Song Huong*), Hue's centre is the Citadel. This is the Vietnamese equivalent of the Forbidden City but it was almost completely destroyed during the Tet Offensive in 1968. It is currently being renovated with the help of UNESCO. Apart from the Citadel, see also: the imperial tombs of the Nguyen emperors and the Thien Mu pagoda with its eight-sided tower, bell dating back to 1701 and laughing Buddha.

Haiphong/Halong Bay/Hong Gai Haiphong is the major northern port; it was badly damaged during the war. Lying on the banks of the Cam River, it can be reached by road or train from Hanoi. The town is within easy reach of some beach resorts of enormous potential, such as Do Son, Cat Be Island and Hong Gai. The latter, with Cam Pha is the centre of the Quang Ninh coalmining industry. There is a resort nearby at Bai Chay which looks out onto Halong Bay—a remarkable scene of traditional junks and rocky karst limestone outcrops and islands which are great for exploring.

I

Indochina A French creation referring to the 1887 union of Laos and Cambodia with Cochin China, Annam and Tonkin. For political reasons, the Indochinese concept has often been more palatable to the Vietnamese than the other two. The Indochinese Communist Party was founded in 1930 at a football match in Hong Kong. It united several Viet factions with the Lao and Khmer anti–colonial struggles under Ho Chi Minh. The first Indochina War was with the French (1946-54), the second against the Americans (1965-73) and the third between Vietnam and Pol Pot's Cambodia.

J

Japanese Occupation Without leaving many traces, the Japanese occupied Vietnam between 1941 and 1945. Until they took full control in March 1945, the day-to-day running was left almost entirely to a Vichy French administration.

K

Khe Sanh Situated on Highway 9 near the Lao border, this highland area was the setting of an infamous siege in late 1967, early '68 which turned out to be a humiliation for the Americans. It was essentially a ploy to reduce the defences of the southern forces prior to the massive Tet Offensive.

L

Lien Xo The Vietnamese word for Russian. Most people will think you are one because that's all they have seen in the past few years. Expect to hear it shouted at you (in fun) as you walk down the street.

Le Loi The main street in Ho Chi Minh City, named after the fifteenth-century national hero who led a peasant army into battle against the Chinese in 1427. Having seen off twenty years of Ming rule, he set up the Le dynasty and in traditional Vietnamese fashion paid homage and tribute to China.

Lang Son The most familiar brand of Vietnamese fire water, otherwise known as rice wine.

M

Mekong Delta Often referred to as the 'Wild West' of Vietnam—probably because it was only populated relatively recently and still has something of a frontier mentality.

The present government is the first to control it fully. The Delta used to be known for its secret societies, spiritual dabbling, private armies, religious sects, smuggling, piracy etc. It is a vast expanse of flat alluvial land with a maze of canals and irrigation waterways. The area is densely populated and is the rice bowl and orchard of the south. Major towns include Can Tho, My Tho, Vinh Long, Long Xuyen and Chau Doc. The mighty Mekong, which is on its way from Cambodia to the South China Sea, divides into four branches.

My Lai Scene of the massacre of over 500 innocent villagers in 1968. This was one of the saddest moments in America's long and vexed involvement in Vietnam. There is a museum in the village which is now known as Son My, near Quang Ngai.

Minerals Northern Vietnam is endowed with sizeable deposits of coal, iron ore, tin and other minerals. Significant oil finds have been made at various offshore locations.

MIAs Soldiers 'Missing In Action'. They are presumed dead, or rather more dubiously, still in captivity. The Americans continue to be obsessed about this issue. Be careful of tricksters offering to show you MIAs in return for a fee.

N

Nha Trang Attractive resort town in Phu Kanh province in an area with some of Vietnam's most stunningly beautiful beaches and coastal scenery. Nearby is Cam Ranh Bay, the controversial naval and air base. See in particular the old Pasteur Institute, Oceanography Institute, Truong Xuan hot springs, Long Son Pagoda (in memory of the monk suicide incident) and Po Nagar, a famous Cham tower.

Nuoc Chanh The ubiquitous Vietnamese drink aside from tea and coffee. Lemon juice served with ice and sugar (plenty of both).

Northern Highlands A remote area stretching from the upper portion of the Red River eastward to the Gulf of Tonkin coast.

Number 1 and Number 10 Old wartime expressions from the south, meaning good and bad.

New Economic Zones This post-war plan aimed to relocate people back into the countryside and out of the swollen towns. The scheme was often heavy handed in practice and became very unpopular.

Ngo Dinh Diem The first President of South Vietnam after the Geneva Conference. Established a dynasty with his detested brother Nhu and sister-in-law Madame Nhu. An old style oriental despot, he was pro–Catholic and fanatically anti-Communist. He and his brother were murdered during a coup in November 1963.

Nam Dinh/Ninh Binh Two towns southeast of Hanoi in an area strewn with limestone outcrops. Visit Loa Lu, the capital of Dai Viet from AD968 until the Ly dynasty chose Thanh Long (Hanoi) in AD1010. Temples of the two Hoan kings can still be visited. Steam trains are still in use on the lines of this region.

Nguyen The family name, it seems, of every other Vietnamese! An old dynastic name. The first Nguyens hailed from the south—from 1675 until the Tay Son rebellion. The second, from 1802 until Bao Dai ruled the whole country, but with the French for the latter half. Among the Nguyen emperors were Gia Long, Minh Mang, Tu Duc, Thieu Tri, Ham Nghi, Dong Khanh, Khai Dinh and Bao Dai.

Nguyen Hue The Robin Hood of Vietnam, he was one of the three brothers who led the Tay Son rebellion. At the age of 23 he defeated the Nguyen lords and Siamese, and by 30 he had beaten the Trinh lords and Chinese–backed Le King. A military genius who died before he could really enjoy the fruits of his victory.

National Liberation Front (NLF) The southern resistance to the Saigon government who fought alongside the NVA. The distinction was often blurred though—the two being referred to collectively as Vietcong.

Nguyen Du (1765–1820) Vietnam's most celebrated poet. His best known work is *Kim Van Kieu*, a 3,254 verse epic, parts of which are on the lips of most Vietnamese children. Much of Du's writing hinted at rebellion against the Confucian system, rural poverty and parental matchmaking.

Nguyen Trai Statesman, poet, writer and accomplice of Le Loi who fought for nine years to finally overthrow the Ming Chinese in 1427.

Ngu Quyen National hero who defeated an invading Chinese fleet in AD938 by planting sharpened stakes into the river bed, and attacking after they floundered.

O

ODP The Orderly Departure Programme is the legal alternative to the Boat People exodus, by which Vietnamese can join relatives overseas. Perhaps sadly, ODP is one of the first English expressions that southerners learn.

P

Phu Quoc An island just off the Cambodian coast which has remained in Vietnamese hands since it was handed over by the French in 1939.

Population Around 70 million, the vast majority of whom live on the coastal plains or in and around the Mekong and Red River Deltas.

Phat Diem Near Nam Dinh, this was a Catholic stronghold and Archbishopric prior to Ho Chi Minh's victory and the Geneva Conference, whereupon an extraordinary exodus took place; 700,000 people migrating to pro-Catholic South Vietnam.

Pleiku Central Highland town west of Quy Nhon. A pleasant town in the middle of a large fertile plateau. Many of its residents are members of the Jarai and Ra De minorities.

Pith Helmet Hat worn by almost all northern men. Made from tree bark and covered with green canvas.

Paracel Islands (Hoang Sa) Disputed between Vietnam and China, these islands lie off the coast of central Vietnam, east of Danang.

Q

Quoc Ngu The transcribed version of the Vietnamese script using the Roman alphabet with a system of tones and accents. It has now taken over completely from Chinese characters—a cultural loss but useful for contact with the outside world.

Quy Nhon/Quang Ngai Two towns on the central Vietnamese coast which became important US bases during the war. Quy Nhon is famous for its performances of classical opera (*tuong*), and is a stopping point for visits to Tay Son and Pleiku.

R

Rhodes, Alexandre de A seventeenth-century Jesuit missionary, it was he who transcribed written Vietnamese from Chinese ideographs into Roman letters, a particularly sophisticated feat, given the period.

Recommended Reading Graham Greene's *The Quiet American* is a must, as is *A Dragon Apparent* by Norman Lewis. For an interesting view of the war from a Vietnamese angle, try *Fire in the Lake* by Francis Fitzgerald, and for a general history of the war, Michael McLean's *Ten Thousand Day War*. Unfortunately, very little Vietnamese literature has been translated.

S

Seventeenth Parallel The point of division between North and South Vietnam as a result of the 1954 Geneva Conference. The Hien Luong bridge marked the exact point. Vietnam had previously been divided at roughly the same place—during the seventeenth and eighteenth-centuries, the Le dynasty had split into two factions, the Trinh lords in the north and the Nguyen in the south.

Sport There are numerous open air *tai chi* and exercise clubs to be seen on the streets at daybreak. Gymnastics are very popular, as are volleyball, badminton, billiards, football, shooting and traditional boxing.

T

Tonkin Name used by the French to describe the northern third of Vietnam, centred around the towns of the Red River Delta. The Gulf of Tonkin is that part of the South China Sea lying between the Northern Vietnamese coast and China's Hainan Island.

Trung Sisters Trung Trac and Trung Nhi are revered as goddesses and heroines. They led the battle against the Chinese and took part in the creation of an independent country which only lasted for two years before the Chinese returned.

Trieu Au The Vietnamese Joan of Arc, she committed suicide in AD248 rather than surrender to the Chinese. Known as 'Woman with the Hanging Breasts', she rode an elephant and led 1,000 men into battle. She was only 23 when she died.

Truong Son Mountains (or Central Highlands) The spinal cord of Vietnam stretching from north to south along the Lao border. Sometimes referred to as the *Chiane Annamatique*.

Tran Hung Dao The great thirteenth-century general who scored three famous victories against Kublai Khan's Mongolian army. His spirit is still worshipped in some parts of Vietnam.

Tay Son Rebellion The village of Tay Son is now known as Phu Phong and can be found in Binh Dinh district near Quy Nhon. It was here in 1771 that three brothers founded a popular uprising against the Le dynasty and its two factions, the Trinh and Nguyen clans. Under the brilliant leadership of Nguyen Hue, they won three battles: in 1785 against the Nguyen clan and Siamese support at the Battle of Rach Gam-Xoai Mut near My Tho; in 1786 against the Trinh lords in the north and in 1789 against the Chinese-backed Le King. After three hundred and fifty years the Le were finally gone, ironically fighting alongside the very country that Le Loi had overthrown in the first place. Nguyen Hue died one year after becoming the new emperor, and his brothers held on for ten years before falling to the French-backed Nguyen Anh. Phu Phong today is well known for its martial arts excellence, and on the fifth day after Tet, Tay Son celebrations take place throughout the country.

Trains Built by the French. The main line runs between Hanoi and Ho Chi Minh City, the journey usually taking around three days. Foreigners have to pay well over the official ticket price.

Tan Son Nhut Ho Chi Minh City International Airport. During the war it was one of the world's busiest, but not anymore! The nearby airplane graveyard has been preserved as an aviation museum.

Uncle Ho Or *Bak Ho*, the affectionate name for Ho Chi Minh (1890-1969). His name meant 'He who enlightens'. His real name was Nguyen Tat Thanh and he had a string of other aliases, the best known one being Nguyen Ai Quoc, 'Nguyen the Patriot'. He was the father of the modern Vietnamese nation and remains a greatly loved and respected figure. Sadly he died in 1969, just before his dreams of 'independence and freedom' were fulfilled.

Viet The dominant and majority of Vietnamese tribes, commonly believed to be of Sino-Indonesian ethnic origin. The Viet first established themselves in the Red River basin (Bac Bo), and gradually moved south over the centuries.

Vinh A northern city in Nghe Tinh which was devastated by American bombing in 1964 and 1972. Vinh has been reconstructed with East German assistance, and parts of it resemble rundown suburbs of East Berlin. Prone to flooding, typhoons and drought, this province and Binh Tri Thien beneath it are the poorest in Vietnam. Sixteen kilometres (ten miles) from Vinh is Lang Sen, the birthplace of Ho Chi Minh, now a popular museum.

Vung Tau Southern beach resort and port (formerly known as Cap St Jacques), which is not as beautiful as many others in Vietnam, but benefits from its proximity to Ho Chi Minh City (two to three hours by road). Could very rapidly become another Pattaya.

Viet Khieu Meaning those Vietnamese who now live overseas. Viet Khieu are returning in increasing numbers now, to visit their families and, in some cases, to do business. They are treated with a mixture of respect, envy and resentment because of their new-found wealth.

Visas Tours can be purchased with associates of Vietnam Tourism in many parts of the world, and a visa is always part of the deal. These tours can be expensive though, so you might decide you want an individual tourist visa. These are issued by various travel agencies in Bangkok and Hong Kong. Some agencies will arrange for you to pick up your visa upon arrival, which may involve an additional cost of around US$25. When you arrive in Vietnam you are also required to register with the police and obtain an internal travel permit. If you are on a tour these formalities are taken care of, if not a travel agency will help.

Weather The north is cold and wet between November and March, hot in May and June, and otherwise pleasant. The south is constantly warm, but hot in April and May. The rainy season lasts from June to October and almost every day there is a deluge around 4 pm—don't forget to bring an umbrella!

Y

Yen Bay Uprising A nationalist (VNQDD) uprising against the French in 1930, followed shortly afterwards by a Communist Party revolt in Nghe Tinh province. Both were rigorously put down by the French and Nguyen Thai Hoc, the VNQDD leader was executed.

Z

Zoo The zoo in Ho Chi Minh City is a pleasant place to visit and can be reached from downtown by boat. It's a shame the elephants have to be shackled on one leg though.